Jane

AUSTEN

Gill Hornby lives with her husband and four children in Kintbury, Berkshire - a place which Jane Austen knew well. This is her first book.

WHO WAS...

Jane
AUSTEN

The Girl with the Magic Pen

GILL HORNBY

Illustrations by Alex Fox

✳ SHORT BOOKS

Published in 2005 by
Short Books
15 Highbury Terrace
London N5 1UP

10 9 8 7 6 5 4 3 2 1

A CIP catalogue record for this book
is available from the British Library.

Illustration copyright © Alex Fox 2005
Quiz by Sebastian Blake

ISBN 1-904095-15-4

Printed in Great Britain by
Bookmarque Ltd, Croydon, Surrey

For Holly, Charlie, Matilda and Sam
With love.

CHAPTER ONE

Everybody knew everybody else in Chawton; it was that kind of village. And soon after the new people moved into the old bailiff's cottage in 1809, everybody thought they knew everything about them, too.

They knew that old Mrs Austen was good for her age. She must have been seventy – not a tooth left in her head! – but she was up every morning feeding the chickens and down on her poor knees all day digging the vegetables. She was a nice enough sort, it was agreed. Always complaining about one ailment or another, but cheerful all the same.

They knew that her husband had been dead for a few years, but her five boys had all done well for themselves, and were very good at looking after their dear old mama. Indeed, the gentleman from the big house was one of her sons and he had given her the lease on the cottage.

And they knew that she was not alone. She had her two daughters living there, looking after her. For neither of them had married – poor things! – though they were nice-looking girls once, you could see that. And they had that other nice spinster, Martha Lloyd there too. She was as poor as a church mouse, apparently: left with nothing when her mother died. The word was that if the Austens hadn't taken her in, she would have ended up a governess...

So, the villagers watched the four ladies going about their daily business. They saw that they lived smooth and ordered lives. Miss Cassandra ran the house with the utmost efficiency, they agreed. In their spare time, Cassandra was always painting or drawing (she was a considerable artist) and Miss Jane would play on her pianoforte (she was a pleasing, though undistinguished, musician). The villagers would glimpse the ladies, in their candlelit window on a winter's afternoon, at their needle-work. They saw them go to church every Sunday, and visit the poor. They noticed that the only gentlemen callers were their many brothers and legions of nephews, and that sometimes the sisters would go off on long visits to them. They could see that they were well into their thirties, had given up all hope of marriage, but were extremely close to one another. They knew that they all lived together in quiet harmony and contentment. So they did know most of it.

There was just one small fact that was kept from the villagers of Chawton. And that was that quiet Miss Jane was a writer. Indeed, she was a great writer: one of the greatest – certainly the greatest woman writer – in the English language.

Jane Austen went to great lengths to keep her own secret. Every morning, she would rise before the others, practise her piano and prepare the breakfast. She would then settle down in the dining-room, at her small, delicate, writing table. And it was here that, on little pieces of paper, in the tiniest handwriting and, with no great show of effort, she produced some of the finest novels ever written. In just eight years, she revised *Pride and Prejudice*, *Sense and Sensibility* and *Northanger Abbey*; she wrote *Emma*, *Mansfield Park* and *Persuasion*. By the time of her death, they were all runaway best-sellers, enjoyed by everybody from the Prince Regent to the ladies of the local lending library. And yet only her family and dear Martha Lloyd knew that she had written them.

Jane relied on the dining-room door to warn her of anybody's approach. At the sound of its creak, she would quickly slide the paper under the blotter so that nobody saw what she was up to. Many of her neighbours were her most avid readers. But they had no idea that their author lived among them.

CHAPTER TWO

Jane Austen's brilliant, short life began at another Hampshire village several miles to the north of Chawton, called Steventon. In 1775, just thirty-eight families lived there, most of them in the tiny thatched cottages which straddled the village green. On a summer's day, when their low front doors were open, you could see the women within, working at their spinning wheels.

At the top of the hill sat the small, plain church of St Nicholas, with the big old manor house beside it. And at the bottom, somewhere between both church and village and settled in its own fields, was the Steventon Rectory.

The Reverend George Austen and his wife had

moved into the village three years before. The manner of Mrs Austen's arrival had made quite an impression. Although she had not been well at the time – quite unable to get up from her bed – she had not wanted to miss the move. And so it was that the Rector's wife had appeared among the people of Steventon reclining on a mattress, which was balanced on a pile of possessions wobbling atop a donkey cart!

George Austen was a handsome, clever, charming man. He loved his family and his congregation loved him. His wife (named Cassandra, like her eldest daughter) was slightly grander than him: she did like to remind people that her grandmother was the sister of a Duke. But, once married to George, she took their constant lack of money in her stride. Two years after her wedding, she still had no other day-time dress than the plain red frock she had been married in.

The Steventon Rectory was a far humbler home than Mrs Austen was used to. It was a basic building, dingy within and horribly prone to damp. There were three main rooms downstairs and seven bedrooms up, plus three low-pitched attics. It sounds big enough, but the Austens were breeding fast.

By 1775, they were already the proud parents of five boys – James, George, Edward, Henry and Francis – as well as their little daughter, Cassy. As a rule, the family did not use its imagination much when it came to girls' names. They all tended to be called Cassandra or Jane, with the occasional Philadelphia thrown in. So when, on December 16th, their seventh child was born a girl, Jane she became. (Which was just as well, given how famous she was to become: Philadelphia Austen is a bit of a mouthful.)

It was a harsh winter that year. The snow fell, heavy, thick and then froze. With February came floods, and the local lanes were impassable. Mrs Austen and her new baby snuggled together in the fug of the four-poster upstairs, and didn't come down for weeks. The boys appeared, chatting, in the bedroom from time to time, and little Cassy – then just three – liked to stay close to her mama. But somehow, the busy household got along without her. It was the fifth of April 1776 before the weather was fine enough for the infant Jane to be carried up to the Steventon font for baptism by her father. Cassandra Austen was a devoted mother to her large brood, but she was – like a lot of women of that time – a little brisk with them. She nursed them all until they were three months old, but once they were weaned, they were out. All their children were farmed out to a woman in the village. One or other parent would visit the infant every day; they did not cut them off . But the rule was that the children were not brought back to the family home until they were able to walk, talk a little and wear proper clothes.

It is hard to say what effect this had upon them. Certainly none of them seems to have formed a close relationship with the foster mother, but they did all grow up to be physically strong and sound. It was so common in those days for babies and children to die from the most routine illnesses. The Austens were unusually lucky: they had eight – they were later to have a sixth son, Charles – and did not lose a single one.

When little Jane returned to the Rectory, it must have seemed a madly hectic place. George Austen was locked in a constant struggle to make ends meet, and was taking on new work all the time. He, of course, had all the duties of a vicar: marrying and burying the people of Steventon and those of the nearby village of Deane, as well as writing his sermons and taking the services. He was also a farmer, trying to get the most out of the cattle and crops he had on his six fields. And on top of that, he became a teacher.

Before his days as a country parson, Rev Austen had been at university in Oxford, and he was a keen classics scholar. It seemed that the best way to educate his own boys was for him to do it himself and why not take on a few other paying pupils while he was at it? So it was that the attic rooms of the Rectory became a small boarding school.

Every year, four or five pupils would come and stay, going home only for Christmas and a summer holiday in august. They slept in the attic with the Austen boys and every morning would troop into the vicar's study, to be instructed in Latin, Greek,

Literature and Natural History. Lunch was shared with the family, and then they were turned outside for games such as cricket and baseball. They put on plays, sang and danced and ran with the hunt through fields and over hedgerows. Every evening, boys and family would gather in the parlour where Mr Austen would read aloud – sometimes a novel, sometimes some poetry, perhaps some Shakespeare. It was, by all accounts, an unusually happy place.

But it must have been come as something as a shock to little Jane. Her life so far had been spent entirely with the foster family down in the village, toddling around on the mud floor of a warm cottage kitchen. Now here she was, transported right into the middle of a boys' school! Her mother cannot have had much time for her. There were generally about seventeen people living in the house at this time. There were servants, too, of course, but only a couple. And somebody had to oversee them. Think of all those meals to be cooked! Think of the sheets to be laundered!

One side-effect of this household set-up was that

the two little Austen girls were flung together from the start. When Jane was born, her father had written that "here was a present plaything for Cassy" and he'd been right. From the moment that Jane returned from the village, she and Cassy were sealed into a little bubble of mutual adoration and understanding that was to last a lifetime. They shared a room, they dressed the same, they were always bracketed together. "Where are the girls? What has happened to the girls?" was George Austen's constant cry, even when they were quite grown up.

It also meant that they both enjoyed an unusual amount of freedom for girls of their age and class. After the boys came out from their lessons, the girls would share their meal with them, then run and tumble after them for the rest of the day. They might join in their ball games, or run up to the road and wave at the stagecoaches, thundering through to Winchester, Portsmouth or London. When it rained, they would all pile into the big old barn.

Later on, when she wrote her novel *Northanger Abbey*, Jane Austen described the "noisy and wild" childhood of her heroine, Catherine Morland, who "loved nothing so well in the world as rolling down the green slope at the back of the house."

The Steventon Rectory, in which Jane grew up, was pulled down long ago, but if you go to the field where it once stood, you can still see the little hill that ran down behind it. Can't you imagine the young Jane, arms and feet outstretched, giggling wildly as she spun herself down into the garden below?

CHAPTER THREE

When Jane was seven, and Cassy was nine, this idyll was shattered. Mrs Austen received a letter from her dear sister, Jane Cooper, to say that she was to send her daughter, also called Jane, away to school. (You see? Everybody is called Jane) Wouldn't it be a good idea if Cassy were to join her?

At the time, it was the custom for the gentry to send their boys away to school and keep their daughters at home. So it was a little strange of the Austens to do the exact opposite. But still, it was agreed. Cassy Austen and Jane Cooper would start at Mrs Cawley's excellent establishment in Oxford. Jane was devastated. How could she live without

Cassy – her best friend in all the world? How could they do this to her? If Cassy was going, then she must go too. Cassy would look after her. What on earth could go wrong? Please, please, please…

Honestly, said Mrs Austen, Jane would want her head chopping off if she thought Cassy's was being chopped off, too. But she quickly backed down. The last thing she needed was little Jane under her feet all day, pining for her playmate and making a nuisance. And after all, Mrs Cawley was, by all accounts, a very respectable woman. The three girls would be fine together. And just think: after years of domestic drudgery, the Austens could have a bit of a break… So in May of 1783, they drove the girls to Oxford, shook the plump hand of Mrs Cawley, kissed their daughters good bye and, with a flick of the horses' reins, trotted off on their first holiday together for years.

The whole episode was an absolute disaster. Mrs Cawley marched the girls round a few colleges, pointed them in the direction of the odd work of art and then, without telling the Austens or the Coopers, promptly moved everyone to

Southampton. Now, Southampton is an extremely busy port, and in those days, there were a lot of sailors and troops arriving from around the world, bringing a lot of germs in with them. An epidemic of "putrid fever", or typhoid, broke out and all three girls collapsed with it. They were wretched; ill and worried. Their parents had no idea they were even in this place, and they felt as if they were about to die. And when Mrs Cawley – that nice, respectable Mrs Cawley! – declared that she thought it best NOT to inform their families of what was happening, they became terrified.

Fortunately, Jane Cooper managed to get a message home to her mama, and Mrs Cooper and Mrs Austen of course dropped everything and rushed south. They found Jane Austen, in the girls' cramped, dingy, little bedroom, unconscious and half dead, and had to nurse her back from the brink before they could take their daughters home to safety. And the story, sadly, does not end there. While caring for the girls, Mrs Cooper caught the disease herself. She died later that year.

***

Jane and Cassy were delighted to be back in the folds of the Steventon Rectory. The crowds of family were now starting to thin slightly, and the pressure on space was easing. Their brother George had been sent to live with another family: he was both physically and mentally handicapped, given to epileptic fits and the Austens had decided that they could no longer cope. James, the tall, fair, clever eldest boy, was taking his degree at Oxford. And now Edward was, rather dramatically, moving on.

Of all the Austen children, Edward's story is the most extraordinary. His sister Jane may have written romantic novels, but Edward actually lived one. Back in 1779, Mr Austen's kinsman, Mr Thomas Knight, had paid a visit. This was a big event for the Austen Family, not because Mr Knight was a close relation of Mr Austen's – he was only some sort of distant cousin – but because he was a rich one. Mr Knight owned the manor at Steventon – indeed it was he who had appointed George Austen as the vicar. But he was rarely there as he also owned a very grand estate at Godmersham in Kent as well as the manor house in Chawton.

The reason for this particular visit was to introduce his new bride, Catherine, to the people of Steventon; there was much excitement at the Rectory and a party was thrown for their distinguished guests. Mrs Knight was delighted by all her new friends, but by twelve-year-old Edward in particular. He was a fair, fine-looking boy, with short legs, a steady nature and terrific charm. Both the Knights fell for him. They were just off on their long bridal tour of Europe. They would be away for months. Would the Austens mind terribly if they took Edward along?

It would be considered a little odd nowadays for newly-weds to borrow a twelve-year old as honeymoon entertainment. It was possibly considered a little odd back in 1779. But, always keen to cut back on her numbers, Mrs Austen readily agreed. The trip was a success and, a few years later, when it became obvious that the Knights were not to be blessed with a child, they returned to the Rectory with another request. Would it be alright with the

Austens if they now adopted Edward as their own? George Austen himself had been orphaned at the age of nine, and was always much more sentimental about his darling children than his wife. Yes, he thought, he jolly well would mind if the Knights adopted him! The boy was an Austen! What about his own family? What, more importantly, about the boy's Latin?

As ever, though, Mrs Austen's approach was slightly more shrewd and entirely practical. After all, apart from George, Edward was the only one of their sons who had no great gift for his studies. The Knights would educate him in useful things, like estate management, and then – more usefully still – they would leave him all their estates and he would have something nice to manage. "I think," she gently advised her husband, "you had better oblige your cousins and let the child go." And so it was that Edward left for a life of Grand Tours, big houses and balls.

Mr and Mrs Knight commissioned the fashionable artist William Wellings to capture the moment of Edward's handover. The picture shows, in silhouette, this young boy in his finest clothes being passed from his real father to his new one. Mr Austen is upright and formal, Mr Knight is casual and relaxed, whilst their wives are seated between them in the middle of a good game of chess! Of course, no mother would go so far as to actually play a board game whilst giving her son away. But the image does show how very common-place adoption was in those days. It was considered a good opportunity for a poorer child, which one could not afford to turn down.

Jane Austen later wrote about adoption in her novels – though never with much approval. The heroine of *Mansfield Park*, Fanny Price, is born into a large, poor family, then adopted by the richer and much grander Bertram family. She has a difficult time with them.

But for Edward, it was like a fairy tale; in fact, it was even better. In fairy tales, people chosen to go off to a charmed life tend never to see their families again. Edward managed to remain extremely close to his and all the Austens were, at some time or another, to benefit from his wealth.

***

Jane spent 1784, her ninth year, entirely at home. After the hideous Mrs Cawley experience no-one dared mention schools again for a bit. Anyway, for a bright girl – and young Jane obviously already was a bright girl – life at the Rectory was education enough.

After all, her home was also a school and, by all accounts, rather a good one. Whilst teaching the boys, George Austen surely let his girls into the study to spin the globe and peer down the microscope. Also, he was a great believer in books – any books – and never a snob about them. There was a fashion at the time for cheap Gothic romances and horror stories, where terrible and ridiculous things happened to young maidens in spooky castles far, far away. There were also rather racy novels, with people having affairs, eloping, coping with drunken mothers, breeding illegitimate children.

If Jane had been born fifty years later, to a Victorian father, she would never have been let near such things. But the cheerful Reverend Austen was as happy for his daughters to read these as the works of Shakespeare, or the Bible. He had an enormous library and, most unusually, he gave his children the run of it. By the time she was eight, Jane was a fluent reader and she was allowed to while away as many hours as she wanted, curled up in his big leather chair consuming any book she could find.

That summer saw an example of what was to turn into a great Austen tradition: amateur theatricals in the Steventon barn. James was home from Oxford, where he was turning into a leading light on the literary scene. In July, he produced *The Rivals* – a hit new comedy by the fashionable playwright Sheridan – with all the boys taking parts and all the children painting scenery, making costumes, tickets and programmes. The performance lasted a staggering five hours, but the dutiful neighbours – the Digweeds, the Lefroys, the Terrys – turned up to watch. It was the highlight of the season and a huge success. Little Jane was quite delighted with it all.

Steventon may have been a tiny backwater of rural Hampshire, but it was a stimulating place for Jane. Her niece later went so far as to call it "the cradle of her genius". Certainly, the Austens were clever people who liked to laugh, and could turn any evening into a party. And much of the humour in the novels of Jane Austen comes from just the sort of witty conversation that would have been the background music of her childhood.

Despite all this, when Jane was ten years old, Mr and Mrs Austen decided to give the formal education of their daughters another chance. This time, Cassy, Jane and the now motherless Jane Cooper were dispatched to the Abbey School in Reading, an establishment built in the shadow of the ruined monastery, where a girls' school still stands today. In those days, its headmistress was Madame la Tournelle – a totally phoney Frenchwoman, who had chosen the name for herself to suggest learning and breeding. When the girls joined the school, they found that she was, in fact, just plain Sarah Hackitt, a woman in her sixties who spoke no French whatsoever and had a cork leg!

Nevertheless, this school was rather more successful than the last. If Mrs Hackitt was not much of a teacher, she was a nice, cosy presence. She gave them bread and butter by the fire every morning, and taught a bit of spelling and needlework. It was by no means a disaster like the last adventure; but the girls were not learning much either. Quite soon, Mr Austen paid up £35 per child for the year, and then brought them home for good.

CHAPTER FOUR

The Christmas of 1786 was a thrilling one for Jane. Her heart thumped as she watched the Steventon pupils bundle their clothes together and drag their trunks up the hill to the stagecoach. For only when the boys had cleared out could the family's visitors arrive, and this year's visitors were going to be too exciting for words. Her cousin, Eliza de Feuillide, had stayed before, but back then she had been plain Betsy Hancock, and Jane had been too young to remember. Eliza was a famously exotic creature who had now made a good marriage to a French nobleman. Jane could hardly wait to meet her.

Eliza had laughing black eyes, a tiny waist and

tales from far beyond Steventon. Her Austen cousins hung on her every well-told story. She had seen it all, from tigers in India, to hot-air balloons over Paris. At a costume ball, she had been close enough to Queen Marie-Antoinette to count the diamonds in her hair. She had wealth, from her godfather Warren Hastings, a title from her aristocratic French husband, and a sweet little boy, who captivated everybody.

So giddy was the atmosphere, that after supper every evening they pushed back the furniture in the Rectory parlour and danced. All the Austen boys fell head over heels in love. Eliza loved the whole family in return, but she liked little Jane best of all. It was the beginning of a rich, lifelong friendship.

At the end of January, the Rectory had to prepare for the new term, and Eliza – and her maid, her mother, her baby and his nurse – had to clear out. The Austen boys watched wistfully as she went – this French aristocrat husband of hers was really most inconvenient! But she promised them all faithfully that, next Christmas, she would return.

In this, her thirteenth, year, Jane was to be left

undisturbed at Steventon. There were to be no hideous school experiments, no near-death illnesses in distant towns. It was uneventful, apart from one small development: she began to write.

Writing was an everyday activity for all the Austens; not just in the form of the endless letter-writing that went on in those days, and the sermons that Mr Austen must produce every week. The Austens also wrote for fun. They were always penning charades and riddles for an evening's entertainment, and the uncles and aunts were often known to communicate in light verse. Great credit is always given to Rev Austen for his encourage-ment of Jane's writing, and that is fair enough. But it is clear from the few examples which remain that it was Mrs Austen who was the parent with the easy talent. Despite her large family, her busy house-hold, her demanding vegetable patch, she always found time to knock out a poem. When one pupil failed to return from his holidays because he was too busy going to dances, he might have expected a stern letter from his teacher. Instead, he got nine witty verses from his teacher's wife:

That you dance very well,
All beholders can tell,
For lightly and nimbly you tread;
But pray, is it meet
To indulge thus your feet
And neglect all the while your poor head?

Jane's eldest brother, James, was busy trotting out lofty verse, in a manner befitting the vicar he was soon to become. He was about to start his own literary magazine in Oxford called *The Loiterer*, full of his own poems and ponderings but also with a lot of chat and gossip about literary life, in which the whole family would take a huge interest. And he loved to adorn the plays he put on at Steventon with his great long prologues and epilogues. There was no doubt, they all said, who was the writer in the family – and James readily (and a little bit smugly) agreed!

So this was the atmosphere in which Jane first picked up her pen. Whatever she wrote was, like everybody else's work, for family entertainment. Its first audience would have been whoever was sitting in the Steventon parlour after supper. It would have been read aloud, and its audience would have wanted, and expected, to laugh. It is no wonder, then, that as soon as Jane began to write, she wrote with a smile.

There are three volumes of Jane Austen's *Juvenilia* – that is, what she wrote as a child. *Volume the First* has her writings from the age of twelve to fifteen: mostly short – extremely short – comic novels. Every one of them was written in the spirit of comedy, and then dedicated to a friend or family member or offered as a present to a loved one.

Frederic and Elfrida is really a short story, but described by Jane, rather grandly, as "A Novel", which pokes happy fun at the romances that were fashionable at the time. A young lady, quite without thinking, finds herself engaged to be married to two different men, so after an excellent supper of partridge, pheasant and pigeon, flings herself into a deep stream.

Its dedication shows that another important person had arrived in Jane's life:

To Miss Lloyd

My dear Martha,

As a small testimony of the gratitude I feel for your late generosity to me in finishing my muslin cloak, I beg leave to offer you this little production of your sincere friend

The Author

Martha Lloyd and her sister Mary had just moved into the nearby village of Deane. Presumably, she found Jane's jokes funny, as they became great friends and were never to lose touch. (Indeed, this is the same Martha who later came to live in Chawton with the Austen ladies when they were all in middle age.)

There are fifteen entries in Jane's *Volume the First* – novels, plays, poems – and not one of them is serious. Sometimes the author lapses into happy rhyme:

> *I am going to have my dinner,*
> *After which I shan't be thinner*

More often than not, she thinks up terrible fates for her heroines, but she never takes them too seriously. *Edgar and Emma* closes with the heroine's heart broken. The narrator tells us quite cheerfully that she "continued in tears the remainder of her life."

When she was sixteen, Jane sat down and wrote *A History of England from the reign of Henry the 4th to the death of Charles the 1st. By a partial, prejudiced and ignorant historian.* Underneath, she added "N.B. there will be very few Dates in this History."

It isn't easy to write a funny history of the Middle Ages, but Jane Austen pulls it off. During the reign of Henry the 5th, we are told, "Lord Cobham was burnt alive, but I forget what for." On Henry the 6th: "It was in this reign that Joan of Arc lived and made such a row among the English. They should not have burnt her — but they did." And under Edward the 4th: "One of Edward's mistresses was Jane Shore, who has had a play written about her, but it is a tragedy and therefore not worth reading."

A History of England is not a scholarly work, but

that last sentence sums up the Austen view: who needed tragedy? They wanted jokes. All the family loved Jane's cheeky romp through the ages. Staunch members of the Church of England they may have been, but they were able to enjoy the idea that Jane saw Elizabeth I as a villain and Mary Queen of Scots as a heroine. Cassandra decorated the manuscript of her *History* with her exquisite illustrations, and had the honour of having the booklet dedicated to her. It became a family treasure that was passed down for generations.

***

When she wasn't being cheeky on the page, though, the young Jane was being the model child in the home. Her brother, Henry, had now joined James at Oxford, and young Francis had been sent off to train as an officer in the Royal Navy. Schoolboys still inhabited the attic, but there was now much more space in the house. Rooms were rearranged so that the girls had their own sitting-room, carpeted in a chocolate-brown.

An artist was paid to coach the talented Cassandra in drawing and water-colour, and an organist from Winchester was hired to improve Jane on the pianoforte. These were both accomplishments which were deemed suitable for young ladies and, indeed, might make them more attractive to possible husbands. Much time was spent on their "work" – that is, their sewing and embroidery – and great care was taken to make the stitches as small and neat as possible, the work very fine. We can still see, on display at her house in Chawton, a present which the seventeen-year-old Jane made for Mary Lloyd when the Lloyd girls moved from Deane to the further village of Ibthorpe. It is a delicate little needlework bag, and was presented with an accompanying verse:

This little bag I hope will prove,
To be not vainly made.
For, if you thread and needle want
It will afford you aid.

And as we are about to part

Twill serve another end,
For when you look upon this Bag
You'll recollect your Friend

The sewing is exquisite, the handwriting small and precise. Indeed, everything about Jane Austen was neat and delicate and particular. It is generally expected, in life stories of great artists, to read tales of rebellion, moodiness and bad behaviour in their youth. But all that can be said about the young Jane Austen was that here was a quiet, well-mannered, loving daughter of a country clergyman who was happily and painlessly blossoming into genius.

CHAPTER FIVE

At around the age of sixteen or seventeen young girls of a certain class in this period were expected to "come out". This was when they were formally presented into society, and able to attend balls and formal dinner parties. It was a big event in a young girl's life, involving a lot of new frocks and the possibility of romance.

For Jane Austen, "coming out" was never an option. Although the Austens were gentry, they were considered a little too far down the social scale to do that sort of thing. It was also an expensive business for parents and Mr and Mrs Austen did not have that sort of money. Besides, Steventon was not like London or Bath. The social life there was mainly arranged around the houses of local families, and anyway Jane had been able to go out locally with her family for a while. So by the time she was sixteen, everyone thought of her as "out", even if they had not seen her "come out".

Jane had a good circle of local friends, whom she saw a lot. She often stayed overnight at the home of Martha and Mary Lloyd. Then there were the Biggs girls – Catherine, Elizabeth and Alethea – whom she would visit in their beautiful house over at Manydown. But most importantly to Jane there was the gorgeous figure of Madame Lefroy.

Anne Lefroy was the wife of the vicar in the nearby village of Ashe, and she was quite a cut above the rest of her Hampshire neighbours. Despite being as English as Yorkshire pudding, she was always known as Madame Lefroy because she was thought to be unusually refined and cultured. She had exploded over the local social scene like a firework, organising great parties and musical evenings and charities. She wrote hymns, rode a donkey, ran a school. She was a fireball of energy. And interestingly, this rare and splendid being recognised something special about young Jane Austen and took her under her wing.

Jane had always been welcome at gatherings at the Lefroy household. And Steventon summers and Christmases were generally enlivened by James's theatrical excitements. But until she was sixteen, she had not been allowed to attend the more formal dances. There were balls every month in the Assembly Rooms at Basingstoke and Alton, and lavish affairs at the local country houses every season. At last, Jane could now go too, have her dance card marked, and find a suitor. Her new life was beginning.

But what was she like, this young girl, as she hit the Hampshire marriage market? What did she look like? And sound like? And say?

The truth is that it is very hard to tell. It is a strange thing, but all the family, at some time in their lives, sat for a formal portrait, at least a silhouette, except for two: George, the desperately handicapped son who lived away from the family for nearly all of his life, and Jane Austen. There *are* two likenesses of Jane by her sister Cassandra, but neither is particularly satisfactory. One is known to be Jane, but is only of her back, so that doesn't tell us much. And the other is of a woman whom people have assumed to be her, but it is not a flattering image, or even a good picture in its own right. There stares out at us a very grumpy, dumpy individual, who looks like she has been waiting far too long for a bus. Can that really be the author of *Pride and Prejudice*?

All the memories that Jane's family have handed down to us are much more flattering. Her niece, Caroline, remembered her Aunt Jane's as "the first face that I can remember thinking pretty". It was round rather than long, with a bright complexion and nice hazel eyes. Her hair was darkish brown, with a natural curl in it. She was not "an absolute beauty, but before she left Steventon she was established as a very pretty girl." One of Mr Austen's pupils recalled "she was certainly pretty – bright and a good deal of colour in her face – like a doll."

Anne Lefroy's brother is the only one to raise a criticism, recalling a face "too full and round-cheeked". But they all agree that she was taller than average, slender and graceful, elegant on the dance floor, and light of step.

So why did the family make no attempt to preserve her image?

Families are funny things, and often cannot see what is under their noses. Jane Austen has lived on as one of the most famous Englishwomen ever born. But to most members of her family, she was always just Cassandra's little sister. Mrs Austen, in particular, thought Cassandra was a wonder — pretty, clever, neat, charming, helpful. Cassandra was her perfect daughter, and Jane was always eclipsed, in her shadow.

Edward, the rather simple but very rich one, also always preferred Cassandra — her conversation was less clever, thank goodness, and she was much more useful around the house. All the Austen boys were now set on their chosen paths — James was a vicar, Henry planned to be one too, Francis and Charles had joined the Navy — and they were destined for success. As for the girls, everyone agreed that Cassandra was the most handsome of the sisters, with her longer face and the excellent Austen aquiline nose, while Jane, somehow, got over-looked.

None of this seems to have bothered her, however. She adored all of her brothers and worshipped Cassandra. When she dedicated stories to her sister, she did so with style: "Your taste is refined, your Sentiments are noble and your Virtues innumer-able." Her tongue may have been in her cheek, but no-one else got that sort of treatment. Besides, Jane had compensations. For all that her mother and Edward preferred Cassy, she knew that her father and her brother Henry favoured her.

George Austen was, after all, a teacher and he had recognised early on that his younger daughter had a rare and wonderful talent. For her nineteenth birthday, he bought her a writing table, costing twelve shillings from Ring's in Basingstoke. Paper was a very expensive thing in those days, but George made sure his daughter always had some. You can tell how precious it was from her manuscripts which still survive: Jane would always correct on the page, rather than copy out anew. *Volume the Second* of her early writings, which contains two much longer attempts at story-writing, plus a few scraps, has written on the cover "Ex dono mei Patris" (A Gift from my Father). He was a constant encouragement to her, and she a great source of pride to him.

But for all that, there was never any doubt where her future lay. The Austens had little money. They lived on George Austen's salary from the church and it was always in the backs of their minds that when he died, his wife and daughters would be left without a home and without a penny. They were not banking on Jane becoming a famous writer or Cassandra a well-known artist. They had no plans for the girls to make their own fortunes. The only hope for the future was that they should marry, as soon and as well as possible.

CHAPTER SIX

From the minute she turned sixteen, it seemed to Jane that marriage was suddenly every-where. Her brother James, now a curate, entered into an excellent match with a local woman, Anne Mathew. She was older than him, and much richer but, as he quickly spotted, she was on the shelf. She accepted him quite promptly and brought with her a much-needed one hundred pounds a year. And Edward – the son who had been adopted at twelve – was courting down in Kent where he now found himself a splendid arrangement. Elizabeth Bridges was just eighteen, very pretty and rolling in money. On their marriage, these two already rich young people became, together, even richer. As Jane was to write later, "It seems that the whole world is in a conspiracy to make one half of this family rich at the expense of the other."

It was perfectly normal in those days to choose whom you were going to marry on the basis of their fortune or their family connections. It was perfectly acceptable to marry in exchange for a nice house. If you should happen to then get on with your spouse, that was a bonus; a free gift. For Jane this was unthinkable. She would – like all the heroines of her novels – only marry for love.

In July 1791, her dear cousin and school-friend, Jane Cooper, took a holiday on the Isle of Wight, and was quite swept off her feet by a passing naval officer. He proposed within the month, despite having no fortune whatsoever, and was happily accepted. That December, Cassy and Jane took the front pew of Steventon church and watched Miss Jane Cooper and Captain Thomas Williams joined as man and wife. Jane was delighted for her. It was just the sort of match of which she approved: based on nothing other than romantic love.

Cassandra would have been watching particularly keenly. It was still a secret, but she had already chosen the man with whom she would spend her life, and there he was at the altar... conducting the wedding ceremony.

Thomas Fowle was a young clergyman and well known to the family. His father, the Reverend Fowle, was one of Mr Austen's oldest friends, and he had sent all four of his boys to the Steventon school. Tom was his second son, a quiet, pleasant, young man, who had known and admired Cassandra all his life. They were now engaged, but quietly so. Tom needed to make some money first to secure the match. They were both sensible young people, who knew the rules. They could, and would, wait for each other until the time was right.

One afternoon, idly waiting for her father to finish some business in the church, Jane began to doodle in the parish register. "Jane Austen to Henry Frederick Howard Fitzwilliam of London," she wrote; and "Jane Austen to Edmund Arthur William Mortimer of Liverpool."

She was beginning to dream. Where was he, this man who would one day come along and take her as his wife? Who would it be?

A few years later, in the January of 1796, Jane felt that she had found him. And where else but at the lovely home of her dear, dear friend Madame Lefroy? That Christmas, a young nephew, Tom Lefroy, was staying with them for the season. He had just finished one degree, and was about to start another. He was clever – training to be a lawyer – and handsome and terrifically good fun. He and Jane met up at every party in the neighbourhood, and he called at the Steventon Rectory in between. They were both falling in love.

Cassandra was away that winter, staying with her future in-laws, the Fowles, at Kintbury in Berkshire. Her fiancé, Tom, had gone to the East Indies for a year or so, as chaplain to Lord Craven. The plan was that, on his return, Lord Craven would give Tom a comfortable living in Shropshire, and Tom and Cassandra could then be married. It was the right thing to do, but the separation was painful. The Fowle family, dear friends to all the Austens, were helping to nurse Cassandra through it.

Had Cassandra been in Steventon that winter, she might have had more influence over her sister. They would have chatted after dances, in their little sitting room with the chocolate brown carpet, and Cassy would have placed a steadying hand on Jane's arm, and warned her not to get too carried away. As it was, Jane was alone, fizzing over with excitement and getting more carried away by the day

We have two letters which Jane wrote to Cassy that January and in both she sounds full of beans. Try as she might not to mention Tom Lefroy, she can't keep his name from the tip of her pen. She is still giddy from the "exceedingly good ball last night", and teases that she is "almost afraid to tell you how my Irish friend and I behaved." When they danced, they danced only with each other; when they sat out, they sat just the two of them, alone. "He is a very gentlemanlike, good-looking, pleasant young man, I assure you... he has but one fault... that his morning-coat is a great deal too light." Which, as she says, can be easily sorted out.

When she writes a few days later, Jane is counting the minutes until the next ball, at the Lefroy's house. She has the feeling that this will be the night: "I rather expect to receive an offer from my friend in the course of the evening." She knows that the romance is the talk of the neighbourhood and that her suitor is being mocked about his feelings for her. She feels happy, pretty, excited; at the top of the tree. On Friday, as she told Cassy, she might be engaged! Imagine it in the parish register: "Jane Austen to Thomas Lefroy". Her mind was leaping ahead to her marriage. Of course, she continued, she and Cassy wouldn't be seeing much of each other now, what with Jane living in Ireland and Cassy buried down in Shropshire. But they could write to each other. And they would have their homes and their families to consume them. They would be so happy, each with her Tom...

***

Six, complete novels have come down to us from Jane Austen. They were written over a long period – around twenty years – and deal with different families and situations. But they have one main thing in common, and that is that they all turn on that moment – the flashpoint – in their heroine's life when she settles on the man she is going to marry. We never see these women as mothers, we barely glimpse them as wives. For what fascinates Jane Austen is that junction in a girl's life where her life changes, and she turns from maiden into bride.

For women who had not been born with their own money, the only protection at that time came with marriage. If you wanted a home of your own, the freedom to travel when you wanted to or even to choose what was for dinner, you had to marry well. It was something which Jane and Cassandra understood perfectly, and for each it was a personal failure.

Jane's romantic adventure with Tom Lefroy ended first, in bitter humiliation. There he was, at the longed-for dance at Ashe House, looking handsome across the floor, but he did not cross it to talk to Jane. There was no dancing, no flirting. He did not propose. She felt crushed. What on earth could have happened to change him like that? The answer lay in Jane's dear, dear friend Madame Lefroy. Anne Lefroy was very fond of Jane, but she was simply facing facts. Her nephew had very little money and excellent prospects. He could do a lot better than this penniless parson's daughter, however clever she was. She told her husband to inform Tom that he would be leaving on the coach for London at the crack of dawn, and he would not be invited back for a while. Jane was given no explanation, and Anne was careful never to mention his name in her presence again. The affair was closed.

Cassandra heard the bare details of the story in letters to Kintbury, and for the rest she had to read between the lines. She felt terribly for her sister, but Jane was still only twenty-one years old. Someone else would come along. And it was not as if they had been engaged...

Meanwhile, Cassandra continued her own patient wait for the return of Tom Fowle's boat.

The following year, a letter came from the East Indies telling her to plan an Easter wedding, which she did with great excitement. Her trousseau was all assembled, but Easter came and went with no news. Then in May, after a long and awful silence, word finally came: Tom Fowle was dead, of Yellow Fever. There would be no funeral. He had been buried at sea.

***

The mishap with Tom Lefroy marked the beginning of a change in Jane Austen. He struck the first real knock to her confidence. She had a naturally optimistic and pleasant nature and her childhood had been entirely sunny and happy. But as she had grown into adulthood, shadows had started to fall. Things had not always been easy for the Austens, and now in particular Jane seemed to become keenly aware of all the insecurities all around her.

England had been at war with France since 1793, for example, and two of her beloved brothers – Francis and Charles – were in the Navy, out there in the seas facing pitched battles and pirates. In England itself, there was a constant fear that the French would actually invade. Those who lived near the south coast – as Jane Austen did – were haunted by the spectre of French soldiers marching ashore. Jane's favourite brother Henry had also joined up as a soldier, and was being prepared to face the enemy. In Steventon, the family waited, anxiously, for bad news.

For their dear cousin Eliza, bad news had come in 1794. France had been in turmoil since the Revolution. Eliza had managed to get out a few months before, but her husband the Count had stayed to protect his property. He was arrested, tried, found guilty of all sorts of things but mostly of just being an aristocrat, and in May he had his head chopped off. Eliza was brave and strong; as brave and strong as you can be if you have hardly spent any time with your husband and he was losing a lot of your money. She managed to smile through her tears, and some people – Henry Austen, for example, and James – thought she looked even more beautiful in her grief.

The following year, an Austen tragedy had happened much nearer to home. James was now a curate and living at nearby Deane, with his wife and darling daughter Anna. In May, one night after supper, Mrs James Austen had felt a touch unwell. A few hours later, she dropped dead. For several days, little Anna wandered the house calling "Mama, mama!" until James could bear it no more. Anna was sent to her grandmother and aunts in Steventon, where she became a firm favourite, especially with her Aunt Jane.

When Jane was twenty-four, there came another dark event in the Austen history – dark, and strange. Mrs Austen had a sister in-law, Mrs Leigh-Perrot, who lived in Bath. One morning, she emerged from a lace-shop after a spot of shopping and was startled to find a rough hand on her arm. She was loudly accused of stealing a yard of lace, which she strongly denied. But on opening her basket, there was the lace inside. The shop-keeper insisted: the woman was a thief, the police must be called.

The most likely explanation for all this is that the shop-keeper had plans to blackmail the Leigh-Perrots, who were rich, grand and childless. But the upshot was that Aunt Leigh-Perrot was arrested and held in jail until the trial could be called. To go through an experience like that was bad enough; the fact that the crime of shop-lifting could in those days be punished by death or deportation to the colonies was something to get really worried about.

All the Austens went into a flap. Of course they believed in Mrs Leigh-Perrot's innocence, and of course, they wanted to show as much support as possible. But then Mrs Austen did the strangest thing. To comfort her sister-in-law in her hour of need, she offered both her daughters to go and stay with her in the stinking, horrible, scary prison until justice had been served!

What can Mrs Austen have been thinking of? She had two genteel daughters who needed to make good marriages. They were only in their mid-twenties; all hope was not lost. What would it do for their prospects to spend a few months in jail? And what about the girls themselves? What a terrible experience for them. The answer, as so often in these stories, may be found in money. The Leigh-Perrots had a large inheritance to pass on, and no children to pass it on to. If Cassandra and Jane went to jail for them, the wily Mrs Austen reasoned, then they would surely be owed a little something when the time came... Fortunately, this story has a happy ending. Mrs Leigh-Perrot refused the girls' kind offer. And as soon as the case came to trial, she was found innocent and triumphantly set free.

But it does show how difficult life could be at the end of the eighteenth century. At one extreme, there was great wealth. Society was very civilised. Good manners were prized. Everyone was very patriotic. On the other side, there was also terrible poverty and great injustice. And the war with the French was taking a heavy toll on domestic life in Britain. It was costing a lot of money, and a lot of lives. Everybody was very worried about it.

Jane and Cassy could see both sides. There was their brother Edward, with his large country estate, his enormous fortune and his growing family. Yet at the same time there was their aunt, locked up with a jailer in horrible conditions for months on end. And what was becoming clear to them was how fragile everything was: how easy it would be to slip through the net that separated one extreme from the other.

***

Life at Steventon was much quieter these days. In 1796, the Rectory had stopped being a school, and it was now back to being a home again. But it was home to only a few – Mr and Mrs Austen, "the girls" and, more often than not, little Anna.

Cassandra was noble in her grief over Tom Fowle. There was no obvious weeping and wailing, she bore it well. But she was different now. Although still in her late twenties, she had taken on the look and the manner of a middle-aged spinster. No longer did she take great trouble with her hair, or pay attention to the latest fashion. She had started to wear a bonnet and a patient look. As far as Cassandra was concerned, Tom had been her one chance, and he was gone. Although she was to live for many more years, she was never again to enjoy a romance.

Jane reacted differently. She was a little quieter after Tom Lefroy left her life; it had been a blow. And there did seem to be such a lot to worry about now. But she reacted in character. Quite soon after Tom's departure, while her wounds still felt raw, she smoothed her skirts and sat down at her delicate little writing-table. And what did she write? A tale of an ambitious young man who leaves a nice girl in the lurch? One where everyone is worried about war and the enemy invasion? A story of husbands having their heads chopped off in revolutions abroad?

No, she did not. Jane Austen wrote to escape from all that. She wrote in order to climb in and snuggle down into a world at peace, where nobody worries about peeling the potatoes and nice girls get the best men. Her stories were gorgeous, sparkling jewels, written to bring joy to both writer and readers. Little Anna Austen recalled standing outside the door of the sitting-room with the chocolate-brown carpet, listening to the voice of her Aunt Jane reading aloud, and the peals of her Aunt Cassandra's laughter in reply. She longed to know what was so funny; years had to pass before she could find out.

It was in that terrible year of 1796 that Jane wrote the novel that was to become *Pride and Prejudice*. Then, in the year of Tom Fowle's death, she wrote *Sense and Sensibility*, about two penniless sisters and their different approaches to love. And, in 1798, their beloved cousin and school friend Jane Cooper was killed by a runaway horse; and Jane Austen wrote *Northanger Abbey*. Perhaps creating these joyful stories was the only way she could cope.

Jane would write busily by day, and read aloud to her family by night. They were delighted with all of these new books, but *Pride and Prejudice* was the favourite of the Austens, as it has proved to be the favourite with the public ever since. It is the story of five daughters, the Bennets of Longbourn. They have a lovely life in a charming house, but are painfully aware that on their father's death they will have nothing. Mrs Bennet is the most terrible fusspot and, quite simply, obsessed with getting her girls married, as well and as quickly as possible.

The eldest girl, Jane Bennet, is beautiful, gentle, pleasing to all and Mrs Bennet has all hopes pinned on her. The second daughter, Elizabeth, is her father's favourite: high-spirited, witty and quite firm in her opinions. Her mother quite despairs of her, sometimes. As the novel opens, a very rich and handsome young man called Mr Bingley moves into the area. Mrs Bennet is beside herself with excitement. And when his even richer and grander friend Mr Darcy comes to stay with him, her ambitions take flight. Unfortunately, in Jane Austen' novels, as in life, the path of true love can be extremely bumpy.

Of all her characters, Elizabeth Bennet seems to be the one nearest to Jane Austen herself, or the one nearest to how Jane Austen would have liked to have been. She was certainly the one Jane loved the most. She wrote to Cassy: "I must confess that I think her as delightful a creature as ever appeared in print." Reverend Austen loved *Pride and Prejudice* so much that he wrote to the London publisher Thomas Cadell, proudly offering it for publication. The rejection came by return of post.

It wasn't such a blow for Jane. We can see in her letters that she was confident about her writing. Her family loved her work, she adored doing it. She was not entirely sure that she wanted it published anyway. Austen ladies, on the whole, did not like to make a fuss. And she was only twenty-five. She still had loads of time. Anything could happen...

CHAPTER SEVEN

One day in December 1800, Jane Austen blew in through the front door of the Steventon Rectory. She had had a wonderful time away, staying with her dear friend Martha Lloyd. Though her hands were cold, her cheeks were rosy until her mother bustled into the hall.

"Well, girls, it is all settled," announced Mrs Austen, briskly. "We have decided to leave Steventon in a few weeks and go to Bath." The shock was such that Jane fainted, clear away, to the floor.

That was how little control an unmarried woman had over her own life. Cassandra and Jane had both been away from home when their parents had made the decision that they would instantly retire and hand the Rectory over to James. They had taken no interest in the opinions of their daughters, who had lived there since birth. Mr and Mrs Austen would now sell all their possessions, even the beloved library! From now on, it would be Bath for the winter, and the seaside in the summer. "The girls" would just have to tag along.

Perhaps the Austens thought that Bath was better territory for husband hunting; that after a few balls at the Assembly Rooms and promenading at the Pump Rooms, they might get these daughters off their hands. If so, they reckoned without the

depression (or perhaps just the sulk) that Jane promptly fell into.

Jane Austen was a highly-emotional woman; great artists often are. She loved her home and her neighbours and the countryside. She quickly became bored with the new social life, wasting time with people she neither knew nor liked. And she never grew to love Bath. She had arrived there in the rain, but then liked it even less in the sun: "It was", she said, "all vapour, shadow, smoke and con-fusion". She moaned to Cassy – "Another stupid party last night" – and ticked her off: "Why did you dance four dances with so stupid a man?" She was thoroughly fed up.

***

The years 1800-1808 were the low-point of Jane Austen's life. During those long eight years, she had no place to call home, she was dragged from pillar to post. She felt insecure all the time.

It was not a bad time for the Austen family on the whole. Her parents were enjoying their retirement.

Mr Austen loved nothing better than a few weeks in Lyme, or Sidmouth. James was now installed in the Steventon Rectory. Edward had taken over the vast house of Godmersham and his beautiful wife delivered a beautiful child nearly every year. And Henry – lucky Henry! – was suddenly the very happy husband of glamorous cousin Eliza. Jane loved her brothers and delighted in their happiness but there did seem to be something wrong here. The more the boys prospered, the more down-trodden the girls became. Marriage was the only answer. Perhaps she ought to make more of an effort...

Jane had never appeared desperate to get married – even if others presumed, from the outside, that she must be. Opportunities had come along, but really she did not see why she should settle for just anybody. The year after the Tom business, for instance, her dear friend Anne Lefroy had made some efforts on her behalf.

Anne had always felt a bit guilty about driving Tom away, and decided she would make it up to Jane – find her some sort of consolation prize.

What she came up with was an insult.

The Reverend Samuel Blackall was brought into Hampshire to stay with the Lefroys and flirt with Jane Austen, who met him with total indifference. He was pompous and unattractive; incapable of making a joke. (He bears a striking resemblance to a revolting creature called Mr Collins, in *Pride and Prejudice*.) Madame Lefroy might think that he was Jane's social equal, but Jane was having none of it. She froze him out, all the way back to Suffolk.

But, after a few years wandering around the so-called "pleasure-spots" of England with her parents, Jane's attitude started to soften. She was indeed desperate now – not for marriage as such, but just for some security and peace of mind. And in the middle of this desperation, she received a very tempting offer. She was staying, in December 1803, with her lovely friends, the Biggs girls, in their beautiful house, Manydown. Also there was the Biggs sisters' much younger brother Harris Biggs-Wither, whom Jane had not seen for years. He was only twenty-one, to Jane's twenty-eight, but he was growing up well. She remembered him as a stammering, miserable-looking boy. But here he was, almost – though not quite – presentable.

One evening, to her astonishment, Mr Biggs-Wither made a proposal of marriage. Perhaps because she was so astonished, Miss Austen accepted. This was, after all, the answer to the Austens' prayers: plenty of money, a great big house, with room enough for Cassy. All in the party were delighted, and the merriment went on till late.

Once she was back in her bedroom, though, Jane's doubts bubbled up. He was perfectly nice, this boy, but they had nothing in common. She would never love him! She couldn't spend the rest of her life with him, however splendid his estate was. She was both perfectly sure she had to get out of this arrangement now, and quite covered in confusion about how to do it. What a frightful scene this was going to make! She woke Cassandra first thing, and told her what she had decided. Together they informed the Biggs-Withers, begged for their coach and bolted. The first thing the Austen family knew of the incident was when James answered a furious banging on the door to the Steventon

Rectory. There on the doorstep he found both his sisters, quite hysterical with embarrassment and shame.

There are many gaps in our knowledge of Jane's adult life; secrets that Jane, or Cassandra, did not want us to know. But whispers have come down to us that Jane did fall in love around this period. He was a clergyman, the story goes, and they were somewhere by the sea. He made her laugh, and loved her back. They arranged to meet again and the romance might have come to something. But he died, suddenly, tragically, young. And so Jane's heart broke for a second, and final, time.

***

For years Jane had been dragging her manuscripts around England with her, although she had never found the peace of mind to do anything with them. But soon after the drama with Harris Bigg-Wither, she returned to her work. She began a new novel called *The Watsons*, about the husband-hunting of four daughters of a penniless parson. It is a rather desperate tale. "But you know we must marry," says Emma Watson to her sister, "My father cannot provide for us and it is very bad to grow old and be poor and laughed at."

She also took out a novel she had written earlier. It was then called *Susan* but we now know it as *Northanger Abbey*. She copied it out and prepared it for publishers. She had had enough of drooping around the place feeling miserable. She was not going to be "old and poor and laughed at". Jane Austen was going to be a writer again.

Her dear brother Henry was encouraging. Henry was different from the other Austens, all the parsons, squires and sailors. He was much more worldly, with a keen eye for opportunity and success. He and Eliza were enjoying a rather dashing life in London, getting through Eliza's money. He decided to appoint himself Jane's agent, and made an instant sale. Mr Richard Crosby, a publisher in London, was the first to buy a Jane Austen novel. He paid £10.00 for it and placed an advertisement in a catalogue, trumpeting this exciting new work coming soon.

But then, on January 2nd 1805, came the worst set-back of all. The Reverend George Austen died, at the age of seventy-four, at home in Bath. His wife and daughters were by his side. It was a terrible loss. Jane's greatest supporter was gone and with him went all means of support. The Church of England had paid Mr Austen a salary in his retirement but, now that he was dead, the money would cease. There was no widow's pension and nothing to inherit. The Austen women were destitute.

The dutiful brothers all rallied round, and each offered to contribute £50 a year. Wealthy Edward gave a little bit, but not that much, more. The women were lucky that the Austen men had such a strong sense of duty to their family. They were often welcome at Edward's vast pile in Godmersham, where they could bask in the luxury of a great country house. And they could stay with Henry and Eliza at their smart addresses in Knightsbridge. But, in between, they had to make do with lodgings, first in Bristol and then Southampton.

Jane's fragile good mood was shattered. Mr Crosby of London, who had sounded so excited about her novel, failed to publish it. He was turning out to be a very bad fellow indeed. And, although he did not want to publish *Susan*, he refused to give it back. He owned it and he would do what he liked with it, which was nothing at all. The whole episode was very frustrating. And now here she was, living in lodgings and in danger of becoming exactly what she feared: old and poor and laughed at.

She went to local Southampton dances, where few men asked her to dance. She joined in local dinners and card games, with people she barely knew and did not like. She set aside the story of *The Watsons*. For the next three years, she wrote nothing more than a letter.

***

It was Edward Austen who finally – and he took his time about it – came to the rescue of the Austen ladies, and changed his sister's life. He owned three large houses and dozens of smaller ones. But it wasn't until the end of 1807 that it eventually dawned on him that he might offer something to his mother. He had a couple of cottages coming free soon, one in Kent and one in Hampshire. Which would they prefer? They immediately went for Hampshire. To be back in the county of their childhood, settled, surrounded by countryside once more! The relief to them all was enormous.

The old bailiff's cottage in Chawton was on the corner of the main village street. It was built in an L-shape, with gardens to the front and back, and windows that looked out over the road to the village duck pond. It had six bedrooms, but Cassy and Jane had shared a room since they were tiny, and would continue to share one here.

Some people might not have liked to live such a busy spot, with the stagecoach to Winchester rattling past the bedroom windows. They were certainly on full view. Mrs Knight wrote that she had heard "of the Chawton party looking very comfortable at breakfast, from a gentleman who was travelling by their door in a post-chaise."

But for Jane it was perfect. It did not bother her to think of strangers looking in. She was just thrilled to find that she could sit there and look out! The comings and goings of a small community were exactly what interested Jane Austen. Once, when talking about her novels, she said, "Three or four families in a country village is the very thing to work on." Dear Edward had provided her with a perfect observation point.

When she moved there in 1808, Jane burst into grateful verse:

> *Our Chawton home, how much we find*
> *Already in it to our mind;*
> *And how convinced that when complete*
> *It will all other houses beat*

That ever have been made or mended,
With rooms concise or rooms extended.

In Southampton, Jane had been an impoverished unmarried daughter and sister; in Chawton, she became, finally, a writer. From the moment this all-female household settled down, the conditions were right. She began to work. And as soon as she finished a book, eager Henry would tear it from her grasp, and rush it up to London.

First, she revised and improved *Sense and Sensibility*. And in 1810, Thomas Egerton of the Military Library agreed to publish it, though the author had to pay for the printing and the advertising. This Henry agreed to do and in 1811, Jane's first book finally came out. The *Morning Chronicle* advertised "A New Novel by A Lady".

A week later, it was "An Extraordinary Novel!". It took a while but, after two years, this three volume edition at fifteen shillings a go, had sold out and everyone was talking about it. Jane Austen had made £140.00.

Unfortunately out of that she had to pay back

Henry for what he had spent in launching her. But the tide was turning. Such was her first success that Thomas Egerton offered to pay her for *Pride and Prejudice*: £110.00 for the copywright. Jane agreed.

1813 was a wonderful year for Jane. *Sense and Sensibility* and *Pride and Prejudice* were hugely successful. She had just finished *Mansfield Park*. The plot of *Emma* was churning in her head. She had good reviews and was the talk of book lovers around the country (although, still, none of them knew her name). She heard that the famous playwright Sheridan – the very author of *The Rivals* which little Jane had so enjoyed back in the Steventon barn – had said that her first novel was one of the cleverest things that he had ever read!

Sadly, that year her dear cousin and sister-in-law Eliza died, but Henry found the perfect distraction in his sister's success. He hugely enjoyed dealing with publishers and organising advertisements. And he was extremely proud of his little Jane. He just wished he was allowed to boast about her a bit more…

She may have been the toast of the literary

world, but Jane was just carrying on as before. Her quiet life in the country continued uninterrupted. She never met with her publishers, or went to a literary party. In fact, Jane never, in her whole life, met another author! She sat in Chawton, writing her books, being with her family, and feeling happy.

In these years her growing band of nieces and nephews were a great source of pleasure to her. The young could often come and stay with their grandmother and aunts, now that they had their own place. And Aunt Jane seems to have been everybody's favourite. She was growing into middle age, but she still loved to play games. Perhaps because of those years of training by the schoolboys, she was excellent with a ball, and would play with them for hours.

Anna remembered how, when she was little, her aunt would entertain her with stories that would last three or four days. Fanny recalled a rainy day in Godmersham, when she played schools with all the Austen ladies. Aunt Jane took the part of Miss Popham the Schoolteacher, and Grandmamma played Betty Jones, the pie-woman. While the favourite game of Jane's niece, Caroline, was called "After the Ball", in which the girl and her two aunts would loll around in their upstairs sitting-room, playing at exhaustion and recalling the dramatic events of a make-believe night before.

Jane Austen was certainly wonderful with children, and would have made an excellent mother. But, in a sense, her books were her offspring and she poured all that love and devotion into every single one. When she was waiting for *Sense and Sensibility* to appear, she said "I can no more forget it than a mother can forget her suckling baby." She called *Pride and Prejudice* "my darling child". And in 1814, during a very cold winter, just like the one when she was born, Jane spent her time tucked up by the Chawton fireside, giving birth herself – to *Emma*.

Mansfield Park sold out like the other two novels, but still Jane kept her authorship secret. There was an old spinster in the Chawton called Miss Benn, or "poor Miss Benn", as everyone always called her. It was one of the Austens social duties to sit with poor Miss Benn sometimes, to keep her company, perhaps read to her. Mrs Austen and her daughter Jane read to poor Miss Benn every word of the exciting new novel *Pride and Prejudice*. Miss Benn was very forthright with her opinions on the story. Perhaps she might have minded her tongue if she had known that her reader was the author!

It must have been extremely difficult at times for Jane to carry on with this secrecy. One of her nieces remembered how inspiration would suddenly hit her aunt: she would be sitting by the fireside, sewing, when suddenly she would burst into laughter and run over to her table and scribble down a note. That behaviour looks just fine from a famous author, but to outsiders Miss Jane Austen must often have seemed more than a little odd!

Even some of her family did not know Jane's secret. One of her favourite nephews, James's son Edward, read and enjoyed *Sense and Sensibility* and *Pride and Prejudice* with the rest of the country. But no-one in his family thought to tell him who had written them. When he was finally old enough to be let into the great secret, he responded in typical family fashion: he sat down and wrote a poem.

> *No words can express, my dear Aunt, my surprise*
> *Or make you conceive how I opened my eyes,*
> *Like a pig Butcher Pile has just struck with his knife,*
> *When I heard for the first time in my life*
> *That I had the honour to have a relation*
> *Whose works were dispersed through the whole of the*
> *Nation.*

As Jane's success grew, though, Henry found it too hard to keep quiet. In Scotland on a visit, the secret burst out of him in a conversation with a few ladies. It started to trickle down south.

Then, in 1815, Henry became worryingly ill and Jane went up to London to nurse him. It turned out that Henry shared a doctor with the Prince Regent. The Prince Regent was a terrible playboy, woefully extravagant and horrible to his wife. A lot of people disapproved of him terribly, and Jane Austen was one of them. Everyone in smart society, however, was desperate to impress him, and Henry Austen was so excited by the connection that he started blabbing to the doctor. The result was that Jane was asked to dedicate her next book to the Prince. Rather tetchily, she obliged:

> *To –*
> *HIS ROYAL HIGHNESS*
> *THE PRINCE REGENT,*
> *THIS WORK IS,*
> *BY HIS ROYAL HIGHNESS'S PERMISSION,*
> *MOST RESPECTFULLY*
> *DEDICATED,*
> *BY HIS ROYAL HIGHNESS'S*
> *DUTIFUL*
> *AND OBEDIENT*
> *HUMBLE SERVANT,*
> *THE AUTHOR.*

His Royal Highness never made any acknowledgement to his "humble servant, the author". Two hundred copies of *Emma* were published in 1816, price twenty-one shillings.

These were the glory years for Jane Austen. From 1808 everything was lovely. She was not very rich, but she had enough to feel independent. Her work was very famous, but she still lived a quiet private life. She had a nice, modest home with her beloved sister and she had the huge fun and satisfaction of being able to write whenever and whatever she liked. But then, once again, it all started to go wrong. Jane Austen did not have much good luck. By 1816 it had begun to run out.

First of all, things started to go wrong with the family. In February, Charles's ship was wrecked. In March, the bank which Henry had opened went bust, taking a lot of family money with it. And Edward was involved in a difficult court case over his inheritance which threatened to lose him a huge amount of money. Despite Jane's success, the Chawton ladies still depended on their allowance from their brothers, and this looked under threat.

Emma had made a wonderful £221/6s/4d (two hundred and twenty-one pounds, six shillings and four pence), but Jane's new publisher, John Murray, said that he had lost money on *Mansfield Park*. He only gave a measly £38.00 to the author. Even at the height of her success, Jane's money worries were coming back to haunt her. She moaned to her niece Fanny: "Single women do have a dreadful propensity for being poor."

In March 1817, came the final straw. Her uncle Leigh-Perrot died. The inheritance which Mrs Austen had been planning on for years went entirely to his own wife. It was a blow which Jane seemed to take unusually hard. She used to be stronger than this. After all, it wasn't the first financial crisis to hit the Austen family.

But the real problem was that for the last year, Jane had been feeling unwell. She did not like to make a fuss, it wasn't in her nature. And as none of the doctors had managed to tell her what was wrong, there probably wasn't anything to worry about. Cassy took her off to the spa at Cheltenham, but it did no good. She was tired all the time, her skin was becoming increasingly yellow, she became too weak to hold her pen.

She had just finished *Persuasion* and had an idea for another book, about a village called Sanditon.

But then she started to get fevers and attacks. Her niece Caroline remembers that, instead of taking to the sofa in the Chawton parlour, Jane arranged two chairs to lie on, so that her mother could still take her nap. But by April, when Caroline and Anna walked over from Steventon for a visit, they were alarmed to find their strong Aunt Jane slumped up by the fireside in her bedroom, hardly able to speak. After ten difficult minutes, they were politely asked to leave.

On 27th April, Jane Austen lay propped up on pillows, in the flower-sprigged bedroom she and Cassandra had so happily shared, and wrote her will. She was the proud author of four published novels which were loved by all who read them. She had already sold the copywright to another two. She lay there and worked out exactly how much she had earned, and what was left to pass on to her beloved sister. It came to eighty-four pounds and thirteen shillings.

Cassandra refused to believe that Jane could not be cured, and found another doctor, in Winchester. This Dr Lyford gave her hope, but he needed the patient near him for treatment. On the 24th May, James lent them his carriage and the invalid was gently laid within it, a blanket tucked around her legs. Mrs Austen stood under the porch of the front door, and watched her youngest daughter depart. Under dark clouds and soft rain they drove. In the warmth of the coach, Cassandra held Jane's hand; her brother Henry and nephew William rode, protectively, alongside it. Jane was worried for them out there: she shouldn't like them to catch cold.

The next few weeks, in lodgings at number 8 College Street, were mournful. Dr Lyford continued to treat her, but the illness worsened. In late June, James wrote to his son: "Her case is desperate. An easy departure from this world is the best that can be prayed for." Cassandra hardly dared to leave her sister's side; Jane was sinking so fast. When Cassandra asked if there was anything she wanted, the answer came: "Nothing, but death." It was not then long before the end.

Dr Lyford called and gave her laudanum on 17th July. At four o clock in the morning of the 18th,

Jane Austen died, in her darling sister's arms. She was forty-one years old. Cassandra closed Jane's eyes, cut off a few locks of her hair and took comfort in the "sweet, serene countenance" of the corpse. "She was the sun of my life," she wrote the next day, "the gilder of every pleasure, the soother of every sorrow. It is as if I have lost a part of myself."

Jane's funeral took place first thing in the morning of the 24th July. Women were not expected to attend such melancholy ceremonies in those days so Mrs Austen stayed, as she had throughout her daughter's illness, in the cottage in Chawton. Charles Austen was now living in Eastbourne and unable to make the journey; James had to come only from Steventon, but felt "the trial" would be too much for him. So alone, Cassandra watched from the window of her lodgings, as Jane's coffin was carried down College Street to Winchester Cathedral. Three brothers and one nephew walked beside her; there were no other mourners.

In the period after her death, Jane's siblings acted in their own different ways to protect her memory. Henry continued actively promoting her books. He prepared *Persuasion* for publication and wrestled *Northanger Abbey* back from the grasp of Mr Egerton. They were published together in one volume in 1818.

Cassandra spent months going through all her papers. Whenever she and Jane had been apart, they had written almost every day. Many of these letters – about Tom Fowle, Tom Lefroy, the clergyman by the seaside – were raw and emotional. Cassandra destroyed every single one.

It must have been James who persuaded the Dean of Winchester Cathedral to allow Jane to be buried there. To have a plaque in a cathedral is normally an honour for a distinguished person and Jane was nothing out of the ordinary, as far as the cathedral knew. Whoever composed the epitaph of her gravestone was giving nothing away. It says:

In Memory of Jane Austen, the youngest daughter of the Revd George Austen... The benevolence of her heart, the sweetness of her temper, and the extraordinary endowments of her mind obtained the regard of all who knew her and the warmest love of her intimate connections...

There is no mention of her books. Her nephew, James-Edward, related that quite soon after Jane's death, a trickle of admirers came to visit her grave. As her fame grew, the trickle became a flood. At last, a verger in the Cathedral asked one of these visitors "if there was anything particular about that lady; so many people want to know where she was buried?" And the visitors were happy to tell him that yes, there was something particular about Jane Austen. Something very particular indeed.......

Quiz

After you've finished the book, test yourself and see how well you remember what you've read.

1. What sound warned Jane to hide her writing away from visitors?
The squeak of a loose floor-board
The creak of the dining-room door
The squawk of her pet parrot

2. Jane's father supplemented his income as the vicar of Steventon by:
Buying and selling second-hand carriages
Writing horoscopes for the local paper
Running a private boarding school for boys

3. Girls in the Austen family were usually called Cassandra, Jane or:
Philadelphia
Pandora
Pennsylvania

4. Jane's first experience of school resulted in:
Top marks in her SATs
A bad dose of typhoid fever
A lifelong love of badminton

5. Jane loved to spend her time:
Reading the books in her father's library
Listening to plays on the radio

Playing football with her classmates

6. As a young boy, Jane's brother Edward was:
Abducted by pirates
Adopted by a rich relative
Arrested for drunkenness

7. To amuse themselves and their neighbours, the Austen family:
Wrote and performed plays and poems
Arranged displays of country-dancing
Organised table-tennis tournaments

8. At the age of 16, Jane wrote:
A biography of Henry VIII
A history of England
A novel about the Knights of the Round Table

9. In the 18th century, young men and women would meet their marriage partners by:
Joining the church youth club
Putting an ad in a lonely hearts column
Going to balls and dances

10. The only drawing of Jane to survive shows her as:
A great beauty with flowing blond locks
A round-faced grumpy person with wispy brown hair
A spotty teenager with a greasy black fringe

11. In 1796 Jane and her sister Cassy were both in love with men called:

Tom

Dick

Harry

12. During the 1790s, people living in southern England were afraid:

They would be invaded by the French

A plague of locusts would eat all their crops

Climate change would cause a rise in sea-level

13. When a rich relation was sent to prison, Mrs Austen wanted:

To help her escape by bribing a warder

To send Jane and Cassy to prison to keep her company

To disown her as a member of the family

14. Jane's father thought the stories she wrote were:

Boring

Rude

Wonderful

15. Between 1800 and 1808, Rev. and Mrs Austen and their two daughters:

Moved to London

Lived in Bath and seaside resorts on the south coast

Travelled around England in a gypsy caravan

16. Jane briefly accepted a proposal of marriage from a man called:
Barry Wether-Haggs
Woody Heather-Boggs
Harris Biggs-Wither

17. Her brother Henry sold Jane's novel 'Susan' to a publisher for:
£10
£100
£1,000

18. When her books became famous, Jane Austen:
Continued to live in obscurity
Started to live like a celebrity
Had her home converted to electricity

19. Jane Austen's best-known novel is:
Pride and Prejudice
Sense and Sensibility
Northanger Abbey

20. Not long after her death, fans of Jane Austen's work:
Flocked to visit her grave
Erected a statue in her honour
Released a hit single in her memory

Key dates

1775 – Jane is born in Steventon on December 16th.

1783 – Jane goes with her sister Cassandra to Mrs Cawley's school in Oxford.

1796 – Jane meets and falls in love with Tom Lefroy. It was in this year, too, that she wrote the novel that was to become *Pride and Prejudice*.

1797 – Jane wrote *Sense and Sensibility*.

1798 – She wrote *Northanger Abbey*.

1800 – The Austens move to Bath

1803 – Jane receives a proposal of marriage from Henry Biggs-Wither; she first accepts him, then turns him down.

1805 – Jane's father, George Austen, dies, leaving the Austen women destitute.

1800-1808 – Unhappy years which Jane spent being dragged from place to place by her parents.

1808 – Jane moves with Cassandra and her mother to the old bailiff's cottage at Chawton.

1811 – *Sense and Sensibility* is published.

1813 – *Pride and Prejudice* is published.

1814 – Jane begins writing *Emma*; *Mansfield Park* comes out and is widely acclaimed.

1815 – Jane's secret is out. The "Lady Novelist" is revealed.

1816 – *Emma* is published.

1817 – Jane's run of luck is over. Despite the success of her books, financial troubles loom once more, and she falls ill. She deteriorates fast and dies in July.

1818 – Her brother Henry arranges for *Persuasion* and *Northanger Abbey* to be published posthumously.